Contents

A Disappearance

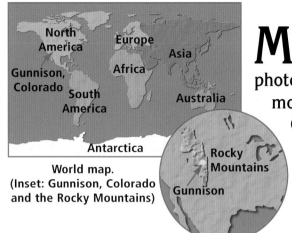

World map.
(Inset: Gunnison, Colorado
and the Rocky Mountains)

Michele Wallace was an adventurous young photographer who had recently moved to Gunnison, Colorado. On 27th August 1974, she set off with her dog for a short camping trip. Three days later, she disappeared.

On 30th August, Michele had finished her camping trip. She was walking back to her car, when she came across two men sitting in a battered old car, drinking beer.

The car belonged to Chuck Matthews, who worked on a local ranch. The other man was Roy Melanson, a **drifter**. The men had met the night before in a bar. Matthews offered to give Michele a lift to her car, and Michele climbed in.

Michele had spent the summer photographing
the spectacular Colorado landscape.

> *This was the last time that anyone saw Michele Wallace alive.*

They reached Michele's car, but then Chuck Matthews' car broke down. Michele said she would drive the two men back into Gunnison.

When Chuck Matthews got out, Roy Melanson asked Michele to drive him to his truck. Chuck Matthews was puzzled. Roy Melanson had told him he did not have a car. Why was he lying now? This was the last time anyone saw Michele Wallace alive.

FORENSIC FACTFILE

A Young Woman Goes Missing

Victim
Michele Wallace

Age
25 years old

Background
Michele had moved from North Carolina to Gunnison, a small town in Western Colorado. She drove to Schofield Park for a camping trip on 27th August 1974.

Date of disappearance
30th August 1974

Eyewitness details
The last person seen with her was Roy Melanson.

Michele Wallace

The Search

Michele Wallace didn't return home after her camping trip. On 2nd September, her mother called the Gunnison County Sheriff's Office to say she was missing.

A huge police search was launched. 400 volunteers searched over 3,400 square kilometres. They found no trace of Michele or her car. Her dog had been shot by a rancher for disturbing cattle.

The police tracked Roy Melanson down to Pueblo, Colorado. He had with him Michele's car, keys, driving licence and camping equipment. He had **pawned** Michele's other belongings.

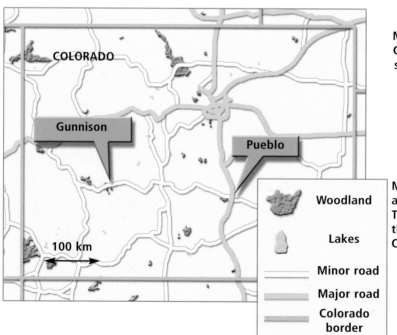

Michele's pet dog was a German Shepherd. After she disappeared, it was shot by a rancher.

COLORADO

Gunnison

Pueblo

100 km

	Woodland
	Lakes
	Minor road
	Major road
	Colorado border

Map to show Gunnison and Pueblo in Colorado. The blue line marks the border of Colorado State.

Roy Melanson claimed Michele had lent him her car after they had a drink together. The police suspected he was involved in her disappearance, but they had not found Michele's body. Unless they could show that Michele was dead, they wouldn't be able to **prosecute** Roy Melanson for murder.

Roy Melanson drove to Pueblo in Michele Wallace's Mazda station wagon.

FORENSIC FACTFILE

The Prime Suspect: Roy Melanson

- Roy Melanson was a wanted criminal. The police knew that he had attacked and possibly killed women in the past.

- When the police found Michele's camera and developed the film, the last photo was of Roy Melanson.

Why wasn't Roy Melanson arrested?
- Nobody can be tried for the same crime twice in the United States. If Roy Melanson was tried for Michele's murder before the police had enough evidence, and he was found not guilty, they would not be able to try him again. This is why the police wanted to wait until they had enough evidence before they arrested him.

Murder suspect Roy Melanson.

The Case Goes Cold

With no sign of Michele's body, the police couldn't charge Roy Melanson with Michele Wallace's murder. However he was sent to prison for a different crime in 1975.

Michele's parents, George and Maggie, and her brother, George Jr, were left with their tragic loss. Five weeks after Michele's disappearance, her mother, Maggie, killed herself.

Roy Melanson was locked up for another crime.

Maggie left a note begging for her daughter's body to be found and buried beside her.

For five long years, the case remained closed. Then, in 1979, hikers in the Rocky Mountains made a gruesome discovery. They found a human **scalp** with two long brown plaits – the same colour as Michele's hair. The police suspected that the scalp was hers.

" Hikers found a human scalp with long brown plaits. "

The scalp was discovered at a fork in a logging road by hikers.

After the scalp was found, the Sheriff's Office reopened the case. However another search for Michele's body found nothing. The scalp was stored in the **evidence room**, and the case was closed again for another 10 years.

The scalp and plaits were mounted and stored in a glass case to keep them safe.

FORENSIC FACTFILE
Cold Cases

- Michele Wallace's disappearance became a **cold case** – a mystery which the police have been unable to solve.

- Some cold cases lie unsolved for many years.

New techniques and equipment are helping the police to solve cold cases.

- In the last 30 to 40 years, new technology used by detectives and forensic experts has led to many cold cases being reopened for fresh investigation.

A Second Chance

In 1989, the Michele Wallace case was reopened for a second time. Kathy Young had recently been promoted to investigator at the Gunnison County Sheriff's Office. She was given permission to work on the Michele Wallace case by Sheriff Rick Murdie.

In the evidence room, Detective Young discovered Michele's scalp and the hairbrush which had been collected from her home when she disappeared. Detective Young sent the scalp and hairbrush to the Colorado Bureau of Investigation for **forensic analysis**. There, the laboratory's Hair and Fibre Analysis team compared the hairs on each piece of evidence. They concluded that they were likely to be from the same head.

Sheriff Rick Murdie of the Gunnison County Sheriff's Office.

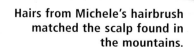

Hairs from Michele's hairbrush matched the scalp found in the mountains.

Detective Young looked into the case further. She found that Roy Melanson was now in prison in Kentucky. She interviewed other prisoners who said he had boasted of killing a woman in Colorado.

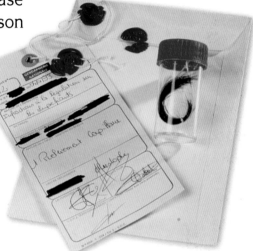

Detective Young also spoke to Roy Melanson himself. He looked stunned when she showed him a photo of Michele's scalp. Roy Melanson did not admit to murder, but thanks to Detective Young there was now more evidence against him.

A sample of hair for forensic analysis.

FORENSIC FACTFILE
Hair Analysis: Part One

- Hair and Fibre Analysis teams work by examining human and animal hairs, bones and fibres, such as threads used in clothing.

- Strands of hair are mounted on a glass slide and put under a microscope for analysis. There are special tests for working out the age, gender and race of a person from their hair.

Forensic scientists examine hairs under a microscope to compare them.

Getting Away with Murder?

Police suspected Roy Melanson of murder, but they couldn't risk taking him to court.

The case was now so strong that Roy Melanson was charged with Michele Wallace's murder. However when the police questioned him, Roy Melanson said he didn't have anything to do with Michele's disappearance. He kept repeating that they still hadn't found her body.

Unless detectives could prove that Michele was dead, they couldn't prove she had been murdered. If Roy Melanson was tried and found not guilty, he could never be tried for the same crime again, no matter how much new evidence police found. If Roy Melanson was ever to be imprisoned and justice done, investigators needed to find Michele's body.

Without a body, the police cannot prove that a murder has taken place.

FORENSIC FACTFILE

NecroSearch: The Facts

Based:
Pueblo, Colorado, USA

Founded:
1987

Mission:
To help law enforcement agencies solve 'unsolvable' crimes.

How:
Necrosearch use a wide range of forensic methods to search for buried bodies, hidden remains and evidence. They also research new ways of finding bodies, and offer to train people in using these methods.

Who:
Necrosearch is made up of volunteer experts. They combine their knowledge of different kinds of science.

Detective Young refused to give up. A forensic scientist who had tested the hair of the plaits told her about an organisation called NecroSearch. It specialised in tracking down hidden bodies to help police. Detective Young decided to contact this organisation.

Necrosearch volunteers use techniques based on archaeology to search for evidence.

13

Necrosearch International

Detective Kathy Young hoped that by calling in NecroSearch, she could give Michele's family one last chance of catching the killer.

NecroSearch is a team of experts from different scientific and investigative backgrounds. The members use their knowledge to find murder victims buried in unmarked graves. This helps the police to catch killers.

NecroSearch use forensic methods to carefully examine each clue in a case. The expert knowledge they bring to a case often results in a breakthrough the police couldn't otherwise have reached.

The members of NecroSearch all have 'day jobs' – they may be university professors, doctors or engineers. They help police simply because they want to see justice done.

NecroSearch have a strong track record of finding the bodies of murder victims.

FORENSIC FACTFILE
Finding Hidden Bodies

The volunteer investigators at NecroSearch are specialists in many different areas of forensic science. They work together to find hidden bodies.

- **Forensic anthropologists** can recognise human bones and discover who they belonged to.

- **Animal trackers** know how wild animals behave. They can predict where bones will have been moved to by scavenging animals.

- **Forensic botanists** are plant experts. They can tell where a piece of evidence has been, by looking at small pieces of plant material, seeds or **pollen**.

NecroSearch use 'cadaver dogs', who are trained to find dead human bodies.

They also use high-tech equipment such as ground-penetrating radars, which can help detect bodies underground.

A New Search

In the autumn of 1991, NecroSearch botanist Vicky Trammell examined the hair on the plaits. She noted that it was sun-bleached. This suggested the body had not been buried but left on the ground.

The hair was also full of needles from specific kinds of fir trees. This suggested the body had been dumped on cool, damp, north-facing slopes, where these trees grow.

The Rockies are blocked in winter by up to six metres of snow. The search had to wait until the following summer.

Finally, on 5th August 1992, the search began. Three volunteers from NecroSearch, as well as Detective Young and other police officers, drove to Gunnison and began an intensive search across the same area where the scalp had been found in 1979.
Thanks to Vicky Trammell's work, they had a better idea of where the body might be.

It was impossible to search the mountains during the winter, because any evidence was buried deep under snow.

That first day the searchers found nothing and felt disappointed. Was Michele's body really out there? Could they ever track it down?

Working together, members of NecroSearch and the police searched the slopes of the Rockies.

FORENSIC FACTFILE
Hair Analysis: Part Two

- Using a microscope, forensic scientists can match hairs from the same person found in different places.

- Hair analysis can also show where that person has been. Materials such as plant leaves, seeds and pollen found in hair can act as clues. In Michele's case, the clues in the plaits pointed to a body lying on the ground, on north-facing slopes.

- Hair analysis can also show whether hair was pulled out in a struggle. Since the mid-1990s, it has been possible to analyse the **DNA** of hair. This improves scientists' chances of identifying who it belongs to.

Scientists can discover a surprising amount from a small sample of hair.

A Skull

The breakthrough came on 8th August 1992. NecroSearch's animal tracker, Cecilia Travis, was walking down a mountain slope when she noticed an unusually large, white mushroom.

A ray of light through the trees hit the 'mushroom'. Suddenly Cecilia Travis realised she was looking at a human skull, with a gold tooth in the jaw. She knew that Michele Wallace had a gold tooth. "It's all right Michele, we know now," she murmured.

Michele Wallace's skull was found lying in the grass. The bottom jaw was missing.

> **Cecilia Travis suddenly realised she was looking at a human skull.**

FORENSIC FACTFILE
Forensic Dentistry

- **Forensic dentistry** is the study of a dead person's teeth. It is useful in a case like Michele's, when a body or skull needs to be identified.

- Forensic dentists can tell whether a skull or tooth belonged to someone who is missing. They do this by comparing teeth to the person's dental records, or to photographs of them.

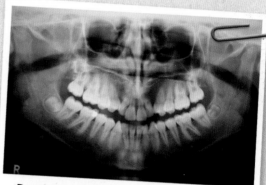

Dentists keep records of their patients' teeth. These records can be used to identify a dead body.

- Evidence from teeth is especially helpful in cold cases. This is because teeth, which are made of a similar material to bone, **decompose** very slowly. Other kinds of evidence, such as DNA evidence, decompose more quickly.

The skull was taken to a laboratory where dental records confirmed it was indeed the skull of Michele Wallace, who had vanished 18 years before.

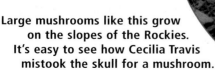

Large mushrooms like this grow on the slopes of the Rockies. It's easy to see how Cecilia Travis mistook the skull for a mushroom.

Gathering Evidence

Working on steep slopes like these can be dangerous.

Searchers spent the next few days examining the steep slope. They were concentrating on the area between the road where the scalp had been found, and the place where they discovered the skull.

The team of police and NecroSearch volunteers used a **search grid** to explore the area in a careful and organized way. Tied together for safety, they searched for clues.

The dotted yellow lines in this picture show how a search grid divides an area up into squares.

The search team found Michele's left boot, with the bones of her left foot still inside.

The searchers uncovered some buttons, some orange thread, and a boot in the grass. The boot contained a sock and 25 bones from Michele's left foot. They also uncovered 15 other bones belonging to Michele's skeleton on the same slope, including six ribs, and both thigh bones.

FORENSIC FACTFILE
Search Grids

- A search grid, or 'zone search', is a way of dividing up an area into smaller zones which are easier to search. These are then carefully searched one by one.

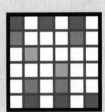

There are several other search patterns detectives use.

- They may use a spiral search. Starting either at the centre, or the outside of the area to be searched, the searchers move around in circles, in a spiral.

- Another pattern is the parallel search, in which searchers form a line and walk slowly forward, searching the ground next to one another.

The Truth at Last

The evidence found in the Rockies suggested that Michele Wallace's body had been thrown downhill from the road. It had fallen onto the slope, ending up next to a tree eight metres below.

This was the expert opinion of NecroSearch's forensic anthropologist, Diane France. Her opinion was based on the location of the bones. Michele's body had fallen down the hill until it reached a tree which stopped it rolling any further.

It was very unlikely that Michele would have been hiking on such a steep slope, near a road. This was strong evidence that Michele Wallace had not died in an accident, but had been attacked by another person. All the evidence pointed to Roy Melanson.

Forensic anthropologists studied the bones to try to find out how Michele Wallace died.

Roy Melanson had a criminal past, and had been violent to women before. He had been the last person seen with Michele Wallace, and had lied to her. He had stolen all of Michele's belongings, including her car. While in prison, he had also boasted of killing a woman in Colorado.

Most importantly, the police could finally prove that Michele Wallace was dead. There was now enough evidence to **prosecute** Roy Melanson for murder.

All the evidence pointed to Roy Melanson.

FORENSIC FACTFILE
Forensic Anthropology

- The science of examining the skeleton or the bones of a dead body is called **forensic anthropology**.

- A forensic anthropologist analyses the bones to identify the victim. Bones can reveal a person's age, height, gender, race, and how they died.

- Diane France found enough evidence in the bones to say they definitely belonged to Michele. However she wasn't able to discover exactly how Michele had been killed.

Forensic anthropology can often tell the police who a person was, and how they died.

The Trial

In February 1993, lawyers met with a judge to explain why Roy Melanson should be tried for the murder of Michele Wallace. The judge agreed, and the trial opened on 23rd August 1993. It had taken nearly 20 years to bring Roy Melanson to court.

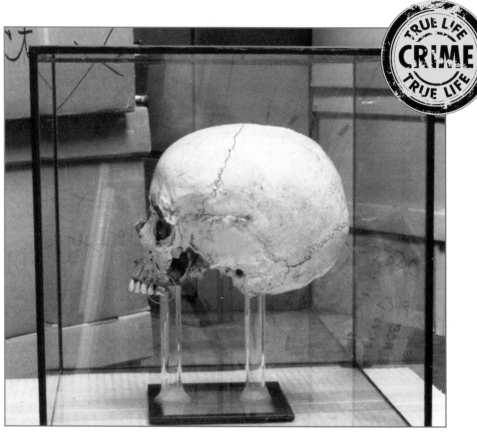

Michele Wallace's skull was displayed in a glass case during the trial of Roy Melanson. Her gold tooth can be seen (circled).

As part of the trial, the **jury** was taken to the site where Michele's body had been found, to see it for themselves. The collected remains of Michele Wallace were displayed in the courtroom. This made a strong impact on the jury. Chuck Matthews, who had witnessed Roy Melanson driving off with Michele, gave evidence against him.

On September 1st 1993, Roy Melanson was found guilty of Michele Wallace's murder. He was sentenced to life in prison.

After five and a half hours of discussion, the jury found Roy Melanson guilty of murder.

FORENSIC FACTFILE

The Murderer: Convicted

- Roy Melanson did not appear in court – he was already in prison in the US state of Kentucky for burglary.

- He had previously claimed Michele had dropped him off at a bar in Gunnison, but the evidence against him was strong enough to convict him.

- Roy Melanson was found guilty of murder and sentenced to life in jail. He won't be **eligible** for **parole** until 2012.

Roy Melanson will spend at least 19 years in prison for the murder of Michele Wallace.

Case Closed

30th August 1974

Michele Wallace, a 25-year-old photographer, vanished in the wilderness of the Rocky Mountains in the state of Colorado, USA. She was last seen alive giving a lift to a drifter named Roy Melanson.

2nd September 1974

Michele Wallace's mother contacted the police to say that she had gone missing. 400 volunteers searched the mountains for her.

12th September 1974

The police arrested Roy Melanson in Pueblo, Colorado. He had taken Michele's car and other belongings.

26th July 1979

Mountain hikers found a scalp with two long plaits. Police again searched for Michele's body but found nothing.

1989

The Michele Wallace case was finally reopened. Forensic analysis of the scalp hairs confirmed, without doubt, that the scalp was Michele's. Detective Kathy Young called in experts from an organisation called NecroSearch to help search for Michele's body.

August 1992

First Michele's skull and then 40 of her bones were discovered in the mountains near Gunnison, thanks to NecroSearch. The position of her bones showed she had been thrown down a slope from a road.

23rd August 1993

There was finally enough evidence to charge Roy Melanson with the murder and bring him to trial. Melanson denied Michele's murder.

1st September 1993

Roy Melanson was found guilty and sentenced to life in prison. It had taken almost 20 years to bring Michele's murderer to justice.

Cold Cases

- A **cold case** is an unsolved case in which detectives run out of trails to follow. All the information about the case is kept on file when it is closed. A cold case may 'sleep' for many years, until new evidence comes to light and the crime can eventually be solved. If no new leads appear, the case may stay unsolved forever.

- Police departments often have specialist 'cold case squads' who focus on uncovering fresh clues to solve cold cases.

- There have been many famous cold cases in history – Michele Wallace's disappearance is just one.

- In the USA, where Michele lived, more than one third of murder cases are unsolved. The longer a case lies cold, the less likely it is ever to be solved. In New York, for example, if a case has been cold for two years, it has less than a one percent chance of being solved.

The television series *Cold Case* is about a police division in Philadelphia, USA, who investigate unsolved crimes.

Bone Detectives

Scientists who study bones to find evidence about a crime are called **forensic anthropologists**. They can help to identify a body from just a skeleton.

- In their laboratory, they examine the bones to find out the likely age, gender, height, and health of the body. The clues come from the development and wear and tear of the bones. For example, a 25-year-old's bones are more developed than those of a 15-year-old, even if they are the same height.

- Forensic anthropologists can also tell if a person was male or female, and their race, from the shape of their bones.

- Forensic anthropologists also look for scars that can identify someone. They check for broken bones that have healed, or scars from surgery.

- Sometimes, an artist will work with a forensic scientist to draw a picture or make a head sculpture of how the person might have looked.

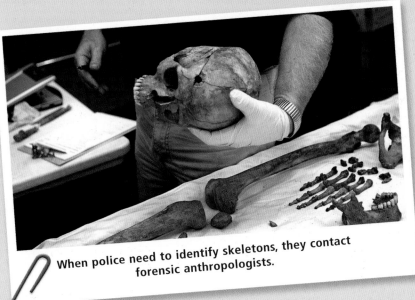

When police need to identify skeletons, they contact forensic anthropologists.

NecroSearch International Limited

- Solving the murder of Michele Wallace was one of NecroSearch's first success stories.

- Since then, this team of forensic experts has helped catch many other killers. They have found many secret graves and solved murders which went unsolved for years.

- They only investigate cases when the police ask for their help. They are not paid for their work. Their goal is to help local people, and victims' families.

- Necrosearch was founded in 1987. Scientists in and around Colorado realised that they had a lot of skills to offer police. They could help them find the bodies of murder victims.

- The name NecroSearch literally means 'Dead Search'. 'Necro' comes from the Greek word 'nekros', which means corpse. In English, when a word begins with 'necro', it means something to do with the dead.

NecroSearch's specialists bring together expert knowledge of various sciences, including archaeology.

Glossary

animal tracker: An expert in following animals. They look for clues like paw prints, hairs, and droppings.

cold case: An unsolved crime which is no longer being investigated.

decompose: To rot or decay.

DNA: A molecule present in many living cells which gives the instructions for making a plant, animal, or other organism.

drifter: Someone who travels from place to place, looking for work.

eligible: To have the right to ask for something.

evidence room: A room where the police keep evidence to do with their investigations.

forensic: Using science in the investigation of a crime.

forensic analysis: Examining evidence using science.

forensic anthropologist: An expert in bones evidence.

forensic anthropology: The scientific study of bones as evidence.

forensic botanist: An expert in scientific evidence to do with plants.

forensic dentistry: The scientific study of evidence from teeth.

jury: A group of people who decide in court whether someone accused of a crime is guilty.

parole: The release of a prisoner before the end of their sentence, as a reward for good behaviour.

pawn: To give someone a valuable object in return for a loan of money.

pollen: A grainy powder produced by flowering plants to fertilise each other.

prosecute: Put someone on trial for a crime.

scalp: The skin of the head apart from the face, where hair grows.

search grid: A way of dividing up an area to be searched into manageable sections.

Index